The Life and Times of

Igor Stravinsky

P.O. Box 196
Hockessin, Delaware 19707

Titles in the Series

The Life and Times of...

Johann Sebastian Bach
Ludwig van Beethoven
Irving Berlin
Hector Berlioz
Leonard Bernstein
Johannes Brahms
Frederic Chopin
Duke Ellington
Stephen Foster
George Gershwin
William Gilbert and Arthur Sullivan
George Frideric Handel
Franz Joseph Haydn
Scott Joplin
Franz Liszt
Felix Mendelssohn
Wolfgang Amadeus Mozart
Franz Peter Schubert
John Philip Sousa
Igor Stravinsky
Peter Ilyich Tchaikovsky
Giuseppe Verdi
Antonio Lucio Vivaldi
Richard Wagner

Visit us on the web: www.mitchelllane.com
Comments? email us: mitchelllane@mitchelllane.com

The Life and Times of

Igor Stravinsky

by Jim Whiting

Printing 3 4 5 6 7 8 9

Library of Congress Cataloging-in-Publication Data
Whiting, Jim, 1943-
The life and times of Igor Stravinsky / by Jim Whiting
p. cm. — (Masters of music)
Includes bibliographical references (p.) and index.
ISBN 1-58415-277-X (library bound)
1. Stravinsky, Igor, 1882-1971—Juvenile literature. 2. Composers—Biography—Juvenile literature. I. Title. II. Masters of music (Mitchell Lane Publishers)
ML3930.S86W55 2004
780'.92—dc22

2004009313

ISBN 13: 9781584152774

ABOUT THE AUTHOR: Jim Whiting has been a journalist, writer, editor, and photographer for more than 20 years. In addition to a lengthy stint as publisher of *Northwest Runner* magazine, Mr. Whiting has contributed articles to the *Seattle Times*, *Conde Nast Traveler*, *Newsday*, and *Saturday Evening Post*. He has edited more than 100 Mitchell Lane titles in the Real-Life Reader Biography series and Unlocking the Secrets of Science. A great lover of classical music, he has written many books for young adults, including *The Life and Times of Irving Berlin* and *The Life and Times of Frédéric Chopin* (Mitchell Lane). He lives in Washington state with his wife and two teenage sons.

PHOTO CREDITS: Cover, pp. 1, 3, 6, 11, 12, 14, 16, 17, 18, 25, 26, 37—Corbis; pp. 8, 20, 23, 24, 26, 28, 34, 36, 40, 42—Hulton Archive/Getty Images

PUBLISHER'S NOTE: This story is based on the author's extensive research, which he believes to be accurate. Documentation of such research is contained on page 47.

The internet sites referenced herein were active as of the publication date. Due to the fleeting nature of some web sites, we cannot guarantee they will all be active when you are reading this book.

PLB / PLB4 / PLB4

Contents

The Life and Times of

Igor Stravinsky

by Jim Whiting

* For Your Information

Even though he was born in Russia, Igor Stravinsky spent most of his life outside his native country. He moved to the United States just before the start of World War II and became an American citizen.

A Night to Remember

The trouble started two weeks before opening night.

When the orchestra members opened the printed copies of the music they would be performing for the premiere of a ballet entitled *The Rite of Spring,* they were stunned. None of them had ever seen music like this. As soon as they began trying to play it, things got worse. The music sounded weird. It was filled with strange rhythms and harsh drumming patterns.

The conductor, Pierre Monteux, had known that the music would be difficult for his orchestra to learn. That was why he crammed seventeen rehearsals into those fourteen days. He tried to be patient, even though he was under a lot of pressure. Each day brought the opening closer. The orchestra had to be ready to play. It didn't help that the composer was by his side during many of the rehearsals, pointing out little things that he wanted to emphasize.

The musicians kept stopping the rehearsals, asking the conductor if there was some mistake. Had their parts been printed correctly? They had a point. Musicians sitting next to each other were often being directed to play different notes. As they continued to badger Monteux, he finally lost his temper.

Pierre Monteux was born in 1875. He became a conductor at the age of 36, and spent the rest of his life leading several of the world's most prestigious orchestras. He died in 1964.

"Do not stop me asking if you have a mistake," he thundered. "If you have one, I will let you know."[1]

The orchestra members weren't the only ones who were confused. The strange rhythms also made it hard for the dancers to match their movements to the music. In addition, the choreographer, the man responsible for telling the dancers what steps to take and when to take them, had chosen to add extra details. That slowed down the tempo and made things even more complicated. Fortunately, the dancers were able to start their preparations long before the orchestra. It still required well over a hundred rehearsals for them to feel comfortable.

With so many people involved in the production—in addition to the dozens of dancers and musicians, there were the stagehands and other technical people—word of the difficulties was bound to leak out. With all this advance gossip, many members of the elegant audience may have arrived at the Théâtre des Champs-Élysées in Paris with their minds already made up. They would love it or they would hate it. And they wouldn't be shy about making their feelings known.

The result was that the premiere of *The Rite of Spring* on May 29, 1913, became one of the most notorious events in musical history.

The composer himself wrote, "As for the actual performance, I am not in a position to judge, as I left the auditorium at the first bars of the prelude, which had at once evoked derisive laughter.

I was disgusted. These demonstrations, at first isolated, soon became general, provoking counter-demonstrations and very quickly developed into a terrific uproar."[2]

If anything, he was understating what happened. "The opening night of *The Rite of Spring* was one of the most riotous in modern musical history, a rock concert gone wild, with people hooting, screaming, hissing, and slapping one another," says author Phil G. Goulding. "Saint-Saëns [a famous composer] rose from his seat early in the performance, made a sarcastic remark, and left the theater in anger. One critic yelled out that the music was fraud. The Austrian ambassador laughed aloud. One man, hissing, was slapped in the face by an irate female neighbor. A society woman spat in the face of one of the demonstrators."[3]

One man became so caught up in the frenzied rhythms that he began beating time on the head of the man sitting in front of him. Another man tied a white handkerchief to his cane and raised it in surrender. An elderly noblewoman stood up in her private box, waved her fan frantically, and shouted, "This is the first time in sixty years that anybody has dared make fun of me."[4] Some members of the audience began to fistfight. Others threw their programs into the orchestra pit.

The turmoil was especially hard on the dancers. "By the time the curtain went up we were pretty scared," said one of them. "The uproar in the audience made it hard to hear even this music."[5]

With waves of noise from the audience crashing down on him, Monteux urged his orchestra to play even louder. The choreographer grabbed a chair and stood on it in the wings, screaming out the time beats to the dancers. Stravinsky stood next to him, furious. "I have never again been that angry," he wrote. "The music was so familiar to me; I loved it, and I could not understand why people who had not yet heard it wanted to protest in advance."[6]

The stage manager began turning the house lights on and off. It may have helped a little. Some of the people who were screaming nasty things when they were concealed by darkness suddenly quieted down when the lights came on and other people could see who they were.

The ballet was in two scenes. There was a brief pause at the end of the first scene while the scenery was being rearranged. The stage manager came out and pleaded with the audience to calm down. He kept the house lights on during the introduction to the second scene. Paris police officers escorted a few people from the theater and placed them under arrest. That made no difference in the overall problem. As soon as the house lights were dimmed, the yelling and the fighting continued. Somehow the musicians and the dancers finally made it to the end. The program had lasted just over half an hour.

As was customary, the composer, the choreographer, and the dancers all made curtain calls. The noise level increased, with supporters applauding furiously and detractors screaming even louder.

The following day, the battle continued as music critics printed their opinions in newspapers. Under the circumstances, it is a little surprising that they had been able to hear enough to even have formed an opinion.

"It was only by straining our ears amid an indescribable racket that we could, painfully, get some rough idea of the new work, prevented from hearing it as much by its defenders as by its attackers," wrote one of the critics.[7]

Some of the complaints were mild. They called it a lack of judgment on the part of an otherwise excellent composer. Others

A scene from Stravinsky's The Rite of Spring *being performed at the Royal Opera House in Covent Garden in London. Compare the differences in choreography and costuming with the same scene on the following page.*

were harsher. Some called the music barbaric. Others dismissed it as mere noise.

The new ballet also had many supporters in the newspapers. One went so far as to call the composer "the Messiah we've been waiting for."[8] Another mentioned the "hard brilliance, the enormous power"[9] of the music. Still others ripped into the audience itself. "Those so-called 'society' people, unable to see, hear and feel for themselves, these grown-up children . . . could only respond to these splendors, so immeasurably remote from their feeble understanding, with the stupid hilarity of infants,"[10] said one. According to another, those in attendance "summed up all the astonishment one must feel in noting the stupid, reasoned malice of what is conventionally known as the Parisian elite in the presence of any enterprise that is genuinely new and daring."[11]

Certainly everyone could agree with the last four words. There was no doubt that this music was unlike anything that had been heard before.

It was composed by a 30-year-old Russian named Igor Stravinsky. Despite the rocky reception that *The Rite of Spring* encountered on its opening night, Stravinsky is considered by many people to be one of the greatest composers of the 20th century.

A scene from Stravinsky's The Rite of Spring. *The ENB (English National Ballet), based in London, has been in existence for more than 50 years.*

FANTASIA

FYInfo

Walt Disney was another man known for doing new and daring things. In 1928, Disney debuted "Steamboat Willie." Starring Mickey Mouse, it was the first animated film with synchronized sound. After this, the art of animation quickly expanded. In 1937, Disney produced *Snow White and the Seven Dwarfs,* which was the first feature-length color animated movie. It was a huge success.

Disney wanted to make classical music more popular. He thought more people would enjoy hearing classical music if it was accompanied by animated action. He brought the two art forms together in a movie called *Fantasia,* which made its debut in 1940. The movie includes eight compositions, each of which is presented with a different style of animation.

The best-known part is composer Paul Dukas's "The Sorcerer's Apprentice." Mickey Mouse, the apprentice, is asked to bring some water for his master. He works hard carrying heavy pails of water. When the sorcerer, or magician, falls asleep, Mickey tries out his master's magic wand. He gets a broomstick to do his work for him, but he can't get the broomstick to stop. He chops it with an ax—but instead of stopping one broomstick, he creates two. Things quickly get out of hand. Hundreds of broomsticks bring pails and pails of water, creating a flood. The sorcerer wakes up just in time to save Mickey.

Fantasia also features Stravinsky's *The Rite of Spring.* The selection begins with the formation of Earth and travels through the age of the dinosaurs. Probably the most memorable scene is a battle to the death between a tyrannosaurus and a stegosaurus. The *Tyrannosaurus rex* is just as fierce and fearsome here as it is in *Jurassic Park.*

Disney was usually a good judge of what the public wanted. He was wrong this time. *Fantasia* didn't do well at the box office when it was released. However, it did become popular during the 1960s. Some people even consider it to be the first music video. Disney Studios released a special edition in 2000 to mark the movie's 60th anniversary. At about the same time, Disney produced a sequel, called *Fantasia 2000.* Stravinsky is represented in this one by his *Firebird* ballet.

Igor Stravinsky conducts an orchestra during a rehearsal. After becoming a conductor when he was nearly 40, he made frequent appearances for much of the rest of his life.

The Budding Musician

Igor Fyodorovich Stravinsky was born on June 17, 1882, in the Russian seaside town of Oranienbaum, now called Lomonosov. Located on the shore of the Gulf of Finland, it is about 25 miles west of St. Petersburg, where his family made its usual home. Igor's father, Fyodor, was the primary bass singer with St. Petersburg's Imperial Opera House. Igor Stravinsky later remembered, "He was a very well-known artist in his day. He had a beautiful voice and an amazing technique, acquired in studying by the Italian method at the St. Petersburg Conservatoire, in addition to great dramatic talent—a rare attribute among opera singers at that time."[1] His mother, Anna, took care of the home and supervised their staff of several servants.

Igor was the third of the couple's four boys. Roman was born in 1874, Yuri in 1879, and Guri in 1884. Both of Igor's parents were cold and distant, and his father had a harsh, often uncontrollable, temper that terrified everyone. Igor didn't like his two older brothers, so his closest relationships were with the family butler, his nurse, and Guri.

His earliest musical memories came during summer vacations in the countryside. One was listening to the peasant women singing

on their way home in the evening after working in the fields all day. When Igor in turn went home and sang, his parents complimented him on how well he had imitated the women.

He also recalled an old peasant who sat on a tree stump. The man was mute, but that didn't stop him from making sounds by clicking his tongue. At first it frightened children such as Igor who weren't familiar with him. Soon they lost their fear, became curious, and sat down next to the man. He had a "song" that consisted of just two syllables, which he would alternate rapidly by clucking his tongue. The old man accompanied himself by putting his right hand under his left armpit, then moving his left arm rapidly up and down. It made a series of small popping sounds that Igor diplomatically said sounded like kisses. He enjoyed watching the man and quickly learned how to imitate him. But when he performed this "music" at home, his disapproving parents quickly made it clear that that was unacceptable behavior.

These first impressions were reinforced when Igor heard his father rehearsing his opera roles at home. He also enjoyed reading his father's operatic scores. He was especially interested in learning about Russia's musical traditions.

A scene from Tchaikovsky's ballet Sleeping Beauty. *This was the first ballet that Stravinsky attended and it made a deep impression on him. His most famous compositions are ballets.*

His musical interests took on another dimension when he attended a performance of Peter Tchaikovsky's ballet *Sleeping*

Beauty. "This was the beginning of two lifelong devotions," writes author Eric Walter White, "to ballet generally, and to the music of Tchaikovsky in particular."[2]

When he was nine, Igor began taking piano lessons. But he wasn't always diligent in following the routine. He enjoyed improvising, or making up tunes as he went along. While his teacher didn't approve, in later life Stravinsky felt that the practice had two benefits. He not only became more familiar with the instrument and what it was capable of doing, but also began to develop some musical ideas. In spite of his sometimes undisciplined approach, he quickly became an excellent pianist and played the music of such great composers as Wolfgang Amadeus Mozart, Ludwig van Beethoven, Franz Schubert, and Felix Mendelssohn.

About this time he attended his first opera. Composed by Mikhail Glinka, it was entitled *A Life for the Czar.* It was one of the scores that he had read in his father's music library, and he had even played some of it on the piano. It was especially exciting for him to hear it being played by a full orchestra.

Mikhail Glinka (1804) was another important early influence on Stravinsky. His operas are rarely performed outside of Russia, but some of his other music is popular today.

An even more memorable evening was in store when he was 11. He attended a performance of *Ruslan and Lyudmila,* another opera by Glinka, for whom he would have a lifelong affection. His father sang a featured role. But that wasn't the main reason for its significance.

"It was my good fortune to catch a glimpse in the foyer [lobby] of Peter Tchaikovsky, whom I had never seen before and was never

to see again," he wrote. "He had just conducted the first audition [performance] of his new symphony—the *Pathetic*—in St. Petersburg. A fortnight [two weeks] later my mother took me to a concert where the same symphony was played in memory of its composer, who had been suddenly carried off by cholera. Deeply though I was impressed by the unexpected death of the great musician, I was far from realizing that this glimpse of the living Tchaikovsky—fleeting though it was—would become one of my most treasured memories."[3]

In later life, Stravinsky became convinced that his musical career really dated from this time. But his path to this career would soon hit a major roadblock.

(Left) Peter Tchaikovsky (1840-1893) is perhaps Russia's most famous composer. Millions of people see performances of his Nutcracker *ballet (below) every year during the holiday season.*

FYInfo

Robert Louis Stevenson and *Treasure Island*

Robert Louis Stevenson

Early in 1882, a few months before Igor Stravinsky was born, the English children's magazine *Young Folks* printed the final installment of Robert Louis Stevenson's novel *Treasure Island.* The story had begun in the magazine the previous October. It appeared in book form in 1883, and Stevenson's career took off. His other books included *A Child's Garden of Verses* (1885), *The Strange Case of Dr. Jekyll and Mr. Hyde* (1886), *Kidnapped* (1886), and *The Black Arrow* (1888).

Stevenson was born in Scotland in 1850. He enrolled in Edinburgh University when he was 17 and studied engineering, the same profession as his father. After a while, he changed his interest and planned on becoming a lawyer. He received his law degree when he was 25. By then he knew he wanted to be a writer. His first two books were about his travels.

During a trip to France in 1876, he met an American woman named Fanny Osbourne. She was married at the time, but she got a divorce three years later, and Stevenson went to California to marry her. They honeymooned at an abandoned silver mine, then moved back to Scotland. Stevenson and his stepson, Lloyd, drew an imaginary treasure map during a rainy vacation. The map stimulated Stevenson's imagination and he soon began writing the story that would make him famous.

Unfortunately, Stevenson had suffered from ill health for his entire life. In 1888, the family started a long trip to the Pacific Ocean. They hoped that Stevenson's health would improve in a warmer climate. They settled on the island of Samoa, where Stevenson wrote several more books. He died from tuberculosis in 1894.

Wallace Berry, Jackie Coogan, and Jackie Cooper in MGM's production of *Treasure Island*

He has certainly not been forgotten. *Treasure Island* is still popular. It has been made into a handful of movies, including serving as the basis for Disney's 2002 animated film *Treasure Planet.*

Stravinsky was very serious about his music. But he also knew how to have a good time. Here he shares a laugh with some friends.

Laying Down the Law

While he may have wanted to put all his time and energy into music, Stravinsky wasn't allowed to. He had to get an education. His lessons had begun years earlier, when he was about seven. For nearly four years, he studied at home with a series of governesses. He passed the entrance examinations to enter a formal school shortly before his 11th birthday, and began his classes soon afterward. He would have been far happier if he had never started. He hated going to school. Moving up to the Gurevich Gymnasium (high school) four years later didn't make any difference.

"I hated the classes and tasks, and I was but a very poor pupil, my lack of industry giving rise to reproaches which only increased my dislike for the school and its lessons," he wrote. "Nor did I find any compensation for all this unpleasantness in those school friendships which might have made things easier. During all my school life, I never came across anyone who had any real attraction for me, something essential always being absent."[1]

His loneliness at school was reflected at home. As always, his parents were cold and distant, and his older brothers didn't want him to bother them. He couldn't even confide in his younger brother because he was afraid of being misunderstood.

Fortunately, he had some refuges. His uncle Alexander Yelachich loved music and encouraged his nephew's musical aspirations. The two of them often played piano duets together. In addition, his father gave him a backstage pass to the theater. Sometimes Igor would spend nearly every weeknight there.

By the time he graduated from the Gurevich Gymnasium, Igor knew that he wanted to pursue a career in music. It was the only thing he cared deeply about. Just as important, it was clear that he had a great deal of ability.

There was a problem. His parents had no intention of allowing him to pursue a music career. They demanded that Igor study law instead. That way he would be assured of having a good job when he graduated.

"As for my inclinations and predilections for music, they regarded them as mere amateurism, to be encouraged up to a point, without in the least taking into consideration the degree to which my aptitudes might be developed," he wrote in his autobiography.[2]

Igor swallowed his disappointment. There was no way he could stand up to his parents, especially considering the violent temper of his father. He entered the University of St. Petersburg in August 1901, enrolling in 15 different law classes. He may have been enrolled, but that doesn't mean that he bothered to attend. He hated the university as much as he had hated his earlier schools. By some estimates, he attended only a few dozen lectures during the four years that he was there.

Instead of studying law, Igor continued his music studies. Within two months of starting at the university, he was taking private lessons in music theory. He made his public debut as a pianist the following month. By this time, his earlier interest in improvising at the piano had gradually expanded to doing formal compositions. His goal was obvious.

"The young law student was writing short piano pieces, andantes [compositions played slowly], melodies, and so on, and was determined, if possible, to break through the barrier caused by his parents' indifference to his musical ambitions," writes Eric Walter White.[3]

His father indirectly contributed to the next step in his son's aspirations. By this time Fyodor was seriously ill with cancer. Accompanied by his wife and Igor, he went to Germany for treatment in the summer of 1902. When they arrived, Igor learned that Nikolai Rimsky-Korsakov, probably Russia's most famous living composer, was vacationing nearby. Igor didn't know him, but he was a good friend of Vladimir Rimsky-Korsakov, the composer's son. The two young men had become acquainted because they were both studying law. Vladimir arranged for his father to meet his friend.

Russian composer Nikolai Rimsky-Korsakov, born in 1844, wrote 15 operas and brilliant orchestral music. He died in 1908.

"I told him of my ambition to become a composer, and asked his advice," Igor wrote. "He made me play some of my first attempts. Alas! The way in which he received them was far from what I had hoped. Seeing how upset I was, and evidently not too anxious to discourage me, he asked if I could play anything else. I did so, of course, and it was then that he gave his opinion."[4]

The opinion wasn't quite what Igor wanted to hear. Rimsky-Korsakov told him that he had a lot to learn. He needed even more private lessons. Igor was naturally discouraged, but he realized that what the older man had said was true. He felt better when Rimsky-Korsakov said that Igor could come to him for advice any time. Even more encouraging, the composer promised to take on Igor as a student when he had learned enough.

Fyodor Stravinsky died late that year. While Igor mourned his father's passing, in a way it came as a relief. Now he could do what he really wanted to do. He even moved out of his parents' house for a brief time, but his mother became seriously ill and he returned.

French composer Claude Debussy (1862-1918). Many piano students learn to play his composition "Clair de Lune," which depicts moonlight in musical terms.

Even though he was still enrolled at the university, Igor began spending a lot of time at the Rimsky-Korsakov home. There he met other young composers. He also began to expand his musical horizons, hearing the works of such men as French composer Claude Debussy (pronounced DEB-you-see) for the first time. Debussy had a new style, in which creating an atmosphere was the important thing. He wrote such works as *La Mer (The Sea),* which gives the impression of rolling waves.

True to his word, Rimsky-Korsakov accepted Igor as a student in 1905. In the background, ominous developments were taking place. After centuries of living under the absolute rule of the czars, many Russians wanted a different type of government, one that took more account of the needs of the people. Early in 1905,

on what came to be known as Bloody Sunday, soldiers fired into a crowd of peaceful marchers, gunning down hundreds. Coupled with a disastrous naval battle with Japan later that year, the incident led to months of rioting. Late in 1905, Czar Nicholas II issued a new constitution that granted a number of basic rights. But many people weren't satisfied. Discontent continued to simmer. Igor wasn't very interested in politics, but the unease did bother him.

He left the university that same year with a partial law degree. Early in 1906 he married his cousin Catherine Nossenko, whom he had known since they were both children. The couple quickly had a son, Theodore, in 1907. Three more children would follow: Lyudmila, a daughter (1908); Sviatoslav Soulima, a son (1910); and Maria Milena, a daughter (1914).

Stravinsky is pictured here with his son Sviatoslav Solima, who was born in 1910. Sviatoslav was the third of Stravinsky's four children. He became a pianist and also did some composing. He died in 1989.

Despite political unrest surrounding him, Stravinsky was doing well. It helped immensely that he knew Rimsky-Korsakov, who assisted him in having his music performed. He also worked on a composition called *Fireworks,* which he wrote as a wedding present for Rimsky-Korsakov's daughter. But the great man died before Stravinsky could show him the piece. Losing his patron greatly saddened him. In some ways, Rimsky-Korsakov had been more of a father figure than his real parent.

Even in death, it seemed as if Rimsky-Korsakov continued to look out for Igor. For when *Fireworks* was performed in 1909, the audience included a man who would change the course of Igor Stravinsky's life.

(top) Three Russian composers include Nikolai Rimsky-Korsakov (left, 1844-1908) who greatly influenced Stravinsky. The others are Anatoly Lyadov (center, 1855-1914) and Alexander Glazunov (1865-1936).

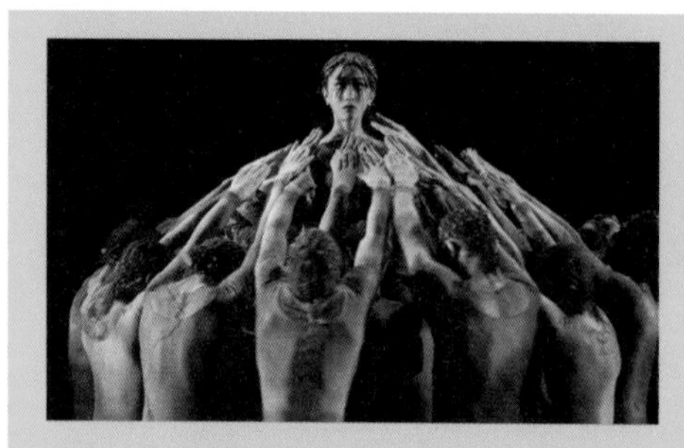

Erina Takahashi (as The Chosen One) in the English National Ballet's production of The Rite of Spring *at Sadlers Wells.*

Christine Camillo in the Berlin Ballet production of Stravinsky's The Rite of Spring.

FYInfo

SERVING HIS FELLOW HUMANS

Albert Schweitzer

While fists were flying in France at *The Rite of Spring* premiere in 1913, Albert Schweitzer was quietly establishing a medical clinic in Africa that would benefit thousands of people. Born in 1875 near Strasbourg, Germany, Schweitzer grew up in a family that put a high value on education and religion. He was also a gifted musician who began playing the organ in public at the age of nine. When he was 21, he made a momentous decision. For nine more years, he would study music, science, and religion. Then he would spend the rest of his life in service to humanity.

Schweitzer became a Lutheran pastor, earned a Ph.D., and taught college. He wrote several books and established an international reputation as an organ player. In 1905, according to his plan, he began medical studies. He received his M.D. degree eight years later. Then he and his wife—who was a nurse—moved to Gabon, a country in West Africa. They established a clinic at Lambaréné. The two most common diseases there were leprosy and sleeping sickness, which caused a great deal of suffering and death.

Four years later, during World War I, the French imprisoned the Schweitzers because they were German citizens. When the war ended the following year, the couple returned to Strasbourg. They stayed in Europe for six years, then went back to Lambaréné. They would remain there for the rest of their lives. Schweitzer used all the money he earned from royalties and personal appearances to expand the hospital. It eventually included more than 70 buildings and had room for more than 500 patients.

For his unselfish dedication, Albert Schweitzer was awarded the 1952 Nobel Peace Prize. He died in 1965 and was buried in Lambaréné.

Despite his apparent frailty in this photograph, Stravinsky was actively involved in many aspects of music. He wrote his last major composition at the age of 84.

Three Great Ballets

Sergei Diaghilev was a Russian theatrical producer who was about to embark on a bold plan. He would present programs in Paris that featured Russian dancers. He formed a company called Ballets Russes, or Russian Ballets. Diaghilev was the kind of man whose motto might be expressed as "think big." He hired the best musicians, the best choreographers, and the best dancers. He was in the theater on the evening that *Fireworks* premiered. The music impressed him so much that he quickly hired Igor Stravinsky. Stravinsky's first job was to score several works of composer Frédéric Chopin for a ballet called *Les Sylphides.* He also began working on a project of his own, an opera called *The Nightingale.*

Soon afterward, Stravinsky got the break that catapulted him to public consciousness.

Diaghilev wanted to do a ballet based on the ancient Russian legend of the Firebird, a brilliant-colored mythical bird. He offered the job of writing the music to an established composer named Anatoly Lyadov. But Lyadov didn't finish by the deadline. In fact, he may not have even started. According to some reports, he had only gotten around to ordering his manuscript paper by the time Diaghilev expected a finished product. Diaghilev was furious. He

turned to Stravinsky, who knew a golden opportunity when he saw one. He quickly completed the score, and *Firebird* premiered in June 1910.

It was a hit. The music was "modern," but it also contained enough traditional elements that anyone could understand it. Even better for Stravinsky, several important composers—Maurice Ravel, Manuel de Falla, and Debussy—were in the audience. All of them were greatly impressed with what they heard. Although Stravinsky had no way of knowing it at the time, his first major composition would become his most popular. In its orchestral form, it is the most frequently performed of all his works. But that was far in the future.

There was no time to rest on his laurels. While he was composing *Firebird,* he had an idea for another ballet. "I dreamed of a scene of pagan ritual in which a chosen sacrificial virgin dances herself to death," he said.[1]

It was *The Rite of Spring.*

He knew that the music would be difficult to compose, so he wanted to work on something else at the same time. With the help of Diaghilev, another ballet quickly took shape. Named *Petrushka,* it is also based on Russian folk tales. Petrushka is one of three puppets who appear at a village fair. He falls in love with a ballerina, one of the other two puppets, but she turns him down in favor of the third, an elegantly dressed Moor. Petrushka becomes so annoying that the Moor chases him through the streets of the town and stabs him to death in front of horrified onlookers. The puppet master tries to reassure them that the "body" is just cloth and sawdust. As he drags it away, the spirit of Petrushka hovers overhead as if in spite.

Petrushka was just as successful as *Firebird.* Within two years Stravinsky had gone from a virtual nobody to one of the most famous composers in Europe. That set the stage for his *Rite of Spring.*

One reason for the frenzied reaction to *The Rite of Spring* was the subject matter. When most people think of a ballet, they have something like Tchaikovsky's *Nutcracker* in mind. *Nutcracker* is certainly the ballet that young people are most likely to attend. During the holiday season, hundreds of productions of the ballet are performed all over the United States. Theater lobbies are filled with girls in new dresses and boys wearing their first neckties. Even though Tchaikovsky was personally a very depressed man, there is no hint of his unhappiness in the music. The melodies are upbeat, bright, and bubbly. Dancers in white tutus and other colorful costumes swirl gracefully around the stage.

Everything about *The Rite of Spring* was totally different. The dancing depicted "the barbaric cruelty of the rites performed by the Russian peasants to celebrate the advent of spring,"[2] observes author Roman Vlad. Many of the movements seemed awkward. Even the costumes were upsetting. Some of the dancers grumbled that they looked as if they were wearing potato sacks.

Stravinsky's music underscored what was happening on stage. It was full of harsh rhythms and employed a great deal of dissonance.

When it premiered in Boston in 1914, a humorous poem appeared in the *Boston Herald.*

Who wrote this fiendish "Rite of Spring,"
What right had he to write the thing?
Against our helpless ears to fling
Its crash, clash, cling, clang, bing, bang, bing?

And then to call it Rite of Spring
The season when on joyous wing
The birds harmonious carols sing
And harmony's in everything!

He who could write the Rite of Spring
If I be right, by right should swing![3]

Of course, no one seriously thought of actually hanging Stravinsky. Yet the poem expressed the feelings of many people.

The novelty soon wore off. Less than a year after the ballet's premiere, Pierre Monteux conducted a concert version. Once again there was a great deal of noise by the time the last note sounded. This time it was deafening applause.

"The entire audience jumped to its feet and cheered," Stravinsky wrote. "I came on stage and hugged Monteux, who was a river of perspiration; it was the saltiest hug of my life. A crowd swept backstage. I was hoisted to anonymous shoulders and carried into the street."[4]

Stravinsky added, "A policeman pushed his way to my side in an effort to protect me, and it was this guardian of the law Diaghilev later fixed on in his accounts of the story: 'Our little Igor now requires police escorts out of his concerts, like a prize fighter.' "[5]

Stravinsky was ready to move on to other projects. He resumed work on his opera *The Nightingale.* It was completed in 1914, and Diaghilev presented it soon afterward. People enjoyed it, but it didn't create the same interest as the ballets.

Events far beyond Stravinsky's control soon intervened. Early in August, the conflict that would eventually become known as World War I broke out. Over its four-year course, more than 10 million people would die. Stravinsky's native Russia would change almost beyond recognition.

FYInfo

THE *HINDENBURG* DISASTER

An air of excitement and anticipation surrounded the New Jersey town of Lakehurst on the evening of May 6, 1937. The huge German airship *Hindenburg* was about to dock after another transatlantic crossing, completing its nonstop service from Germany to the United States. This was the 11th time that the *Hindenburg* had made the crossing, but people were still very interested in the event.

The *Hindenburg* was huge. It stretched 804 feet from one end to the other and 135 feet from top to bottom. Most of the interior of the enormous balloon was filled with hydrogen. Because hydrogen weighs less than air, it lifted the *Hindenburg.* Four 1,000-horsepower motors gave it a speed of 82 miles per hour. The 70 passengers enjoyed luxuries such as a cocktail lounge, library, sitting room with a grand piano, and dining room. A long walkway bordered by large windows gave them excellent views of the earth below them and a chance to get some exercise during the 60-hour flight.

As the *Hindenburg* came into view, movie cameras rolled, photographers took pictures, and radio announcers gave vivid descriptions to listeners all across the United States. Suddenly the rear of the *Hindenburg* burst into flames. Slowly it tumbled to the ground as the fire spread and people began jumping out. A radio announcer named Herbert Morrison gasped, "Oh, the humanity!" as he described the catastrophe. It became one of the most famous phrases ever heard on radio.

Thirty-six people were killed in the disaster. It immediately ended interest in lighter-than-air flight for passengers.

No one is sure what caused the fire. Since hydrogen is so flammable, some people believe that a spark set it off. Others suggest that atmospheric conditions may have ignited the special coating that covered the ship's exterior. Still others believe that it might have been sabotage.

Igor Stravinsky at the age of 79. In spite of physical ailments that required the use of a cane, he was still vigorous as he conducted an orchestra rehearsal.

Leaving His Homeland Behind

As a Russian citizen, Stravinsky couldn't get back home across Germany, which was at war with Russia. The only other routes were difficult and dangerous, so he and his family moved to Switzerland. The country was neutral, which means it didn't take sides in the war and no one could attack it. Many other artists and musicians went there as well. In Russia and elsewhere in Europe, people weren't attending musical events, so there were no new commissions. Money began to get tight.

Conditions worsened in 1917. First Stravinsky learned that his younger brother, Guri, had died. Then during the Russian Revolution the government of the czar was overthrown and a communist government was soon in power. Stravinsky realized that all of his property in his homeland would be taken. It could even be personally dangerous for him to go back home. Under the communist dictatorship, artists and musicians had to create works in a government-approved way.

His problems didn't curb his creativity. He wrote a small-scale stage work called *The Soldier's Tale.* The orchestra was stripped down to the bare essentials, with just seven types of instruments. The composition showed the influence of two American musical forms, ragtime and jazz. It was performed for the first time in September

1918, just before the end of the war. He also completed his first version of *Les Noces (The Wedding),* a series of dance scenes with soloists and chorus set at a Russian peasant wedding (the final version wouldn't premiere until 1923).

When the war was over Stravinsky decided to move to Paris. Although he was exiled from his homeland, he and his family enjoyed much more freedom than Russians living at home. Most important, he could create in the way he wanted.

Giovanni Pergolesi was born in Italy in 1710. He composed a great deal of music in his short life, dying of tuberculosis at the age of 26.

His first significant work after the war was *Pulcinella,* which premiered in 1920. In some ways, it was the opposite of *Firebird, Petrushka,* and *The Rite of Spring,* which had all broken new musical ground. *Pulcinella,* on the other hand, was based on the work of an 18th-century composer named Giovanni Pergolesi. Stravinsky was also influenced by the music of other classical composers. This began what is called his neoclassical period. It would last for 30 years.

While his financial situation had improved after the war, he realized that he could earn extra money by performing his own works, either by conducting them or playing the piano. His first conducting tour started in 1921 and was a great success. Three years later he began performing as a pianist. By 1925 his touring took him to the United States. As he left the ship, he held a brief press conference. A reporter asked Stravinsky what he thought of modern music. He replied that he hated it. Another reporter was confused. It seemed to him that modern music was exactly what Stravinsky wrote. When the reporter pointed that out, Stravinsky said, "I don't write modern music—I only write good music."[1]

For *Pulcinella,* Stravinsky had gone back two centuries. For his next major composition, he went back two millennia. He chose the ancient Greek play *Oedipus Rex.* A king and queen, in order to avoid a prophecy that claims their baby will kill his father and marry his mother, abandon their son, Oedipus, shortly after his birth. The infant, however, is rescued and raised as a herder. As a grown man, he doesn't recognize his father and kills him in a fight. He becomes king, or *rex,* and marries his father's widow—who is of course his mother. Neither is aware of their familial relationship. When the truth finally comes out, his mother hangs herself. Oedipus blinds himself, and condemns himself to a life of aimless wandering.

Premiering in 1927, Stravinsky's *Oedipus Rex* was a mixture of an opera and a concert. The singers appeared on stage fully costumed, but they made little effort to act out their parts, as they would have in an opera. The piece was similar to an 18th-century oratorio, such as George Frideric Handel's famous *Messiah.* Yet there was no mistaking some of the same harsh rhythms that Stravinsky had used so effectively in *The Rite of Spring.*

George Frideric Handel (1685-1759) was born in Germany but lived much of his life in England. He is most famous for writing the oratorio Messiah.

Another unusual feature was that the words were all in Latin. Because Latin was the language in which the Catholic Church conducted many of its rites, the opera almost automatically took on a religious meaning. This also reflected Stravinsky's increasing interest in religion.

His 1928 ballet *Apollon Musagète* marked the beginning of what would prove to be a long relationship with a young Russian choreographer who was also from St. Petersburg.

"George Balanchine, as ballet-master, had arranged the dances exactly as I had wished," Stravinsky wrote. "He had no difficulty in grasping the smallest details of my music, and his beautiful choreography clearly expressed my meaning."[2]

Stravinsky had gained a friend and collaborator. He lost one the following year when Sergei Diaghilev died.

The interest in religion he had shown with *Oedipus Rex* became even more apparent in 1930 with his next major work, *Symphony of Psalms.* It was also in Latin, with words taken directly from the Bible. Again Stravinsky used a mixture of his modern music with older forms, this time going back to the medieval period.

The next years were productive and prosperous for Stravinsky. His works were performed regularly, and financial worries were a distant memory. He even became a French citizen. But on the horizon, storm clouds were building.

The clouds began bursting late in 1938. Stravinsky's daughter Lyudmila and his wife, Catherine, died of tuberculosis within a few months of each other. Then his mother died.

His personal tragedy was reflected in much larger developments. Since coming to power in 1933, German dictator Adolf Hitler had become more and more dangerous. Under his orders, the German army invaded Poland on September 1, 1939. France and Great Britain had pledged to come to the aid of Poland if it was attacked. There was little they could to do help as Hitler conquered Poland in a few weeks. Once again the continent was plunged into warfare. Stravinsky knew that France was squarely in Hitler's crosshairs.

Fortunately, Stravinsky had a way out. He received an invitation to deliver a series of lectures at Harvard University. He left France and crossed the Atlantic Ocean to the safety of the United States.

By then, he was starting to feel that he was more appreciated there than he was in Europe. With so much of his family gone and Hitler in control of much of Europe, there was little reason for him to return. He decided to stay in the United States and moved to Hollywood. He soon regained a great deal of personal happiness when he married an actress and painter named Vera de Bosset, a longtime friend. Living in Hollywood, it wasn't surprising that Stravinsky received many offers to write musical scores for movies. For a variety of reasons, very few of them worked out.

In 1942, he composed *Circus Polka,* one of his most unusual works. It was a ballet commissioned by the world-famous Barnum and Bailey Circus for use during their performances at New York's Madison Square Garden. Barnum and Bailey showed the importance they gave the ballet by hiring the prestigious George Balanchine to do the choreography. The performers all wore tutus, the short ballet skirts that flare out around the dancers' waists. The unusual part was the performers themselves. They were baby elephants! The music was lively and upbeat, and it closed with a rousing series of foot-stomps that may have shaken some of the nearby spectators. Not surprisingly, *Circus Polka* immediately became an audience favorite and was performed hundreds of times.

Stravinsky marked the end of World War II in 1945 with two significant achievements. One was his *Symphony in Three Movements,* which celebrated the return of peace. The other was his becoming a U.S. citizen.

His next major composition came as the result of a visit to the Chicago Art Institute in 1947. He saw an exhibition of humorous drawings called *A Rake's Progress* by famous 18th-century cartoonist William Hogarth. The drawings told the story of a man living in London who lost all his money and became a drunk. Stravinsky thought the story would make a good opera. An American poet named W. H. Auden and writer Chester Kallman wrote the

William Hogarth (1697-1764) was an English artist who was very successful during his lifetime.

libretto, or words, to the opera. Similar in structure to the operas of Wolfgang Amadeus Mozart, *The Rake's Progress* premiered in 1951. It was his final neoclassical work.

Stravinsky had one final turn in his twisting career path. Just after starting *Rake's Progress,* he met a young musician named Robert Craft. Craft soon became Stravinsky's personal assistant and close friend. He persuaded Stravinsky to begin composing yet another type of music: 12-tone, or serial, music.

Western music uses what is known as a chromatic scale, which divides an octave—8 whole notes—into 12 tones. Nearly all of the music with which we are familiar is based on a home key, the tone from which the melody begins and to which it returns. Any tone can serve as the home key. Each key uses only eight tones in the familiar "do-re-mi" pattern.

Serial music, on the other hand, doesn't have a home key and freely uses all 12 tones on the scale. It sounds strange to most people and has little appeal for them. Among professional musicians, however, it is much more important. Men such as Arnold Schoenberg and Alban Berg wrote a great deal of serial music. Soon Stravinsky did too. Most of it was religious music or music in honor of various people.

In 1962, at the age of 80, Stravinsky received an invitation from the government of the Soviet Union (which included Russia) to return to his homeland. He had been gone for 48 years. While he was opposed to the communist government of the Soviet Union, Russia was still the land of his birth. Every place he went, he was

enthusiastically welcomed and made to feel at home. When he visited Leningrad (which St. Petersburg was called at that time), an old man rushed up to him. At first Stravinsky didn't recognize him. It was his old friend Vladimir Rimsky-Korsakov. In an interesting coincidence, Vladimir was living in the same apartment that Stravinsky had occupied more than 50 years earlier while he was writing *Firebird.* The three weeks he spent visiting Russia was probably one of the best experiences of his life.

By then, Stravinsky was starting to show the effects of advancing age. His last major composition, finished in 1966, was the *Requiem Canticles,* written for soloists, a chorus, and full orchestra. While he was working on it, he had the feeling that it was the music that would be played at his funeral. He moved to New York to take advantage of good medical care there. He died in New York on April 6, 1971. Soon afterward, his body was flown to Venice, Italy. His coffin was placed on a wooden gondola and, accompanied by a Russian Orthodox priest, rowed across the lagoon of Venice to the tiny island of San Michele. He was buried a few feet away from his friend Sergei Diaghilev. One of the most remarkable and varied careers in musical history had come to an end.

"Perhaps no other composer in this century—or any—has written in such a variety of styles," notes England's Danceworks School. "And it is the unique genius of Stravinsky that his musical personality is detectable in each of these styles."[3]

Harold Schonberg adds, "Minor composers may achieve great popularity in their day, but they never influence the course of music. Stravinsky did. He was always at the end of the rope, pulling everybody along with him."[4]

Almost everything that he wrote has been recorded. Yet except for the three great ballets that he composed at the start of his career—*Firebird, Petrushka,* and *The Rite of Spring*—and to a lesser

Left: John Martin Harvey in the title role of Oedipus Rex. *The story is about a man who accidentally kills his father and marries his mother.*

RIght: Ballerina Tamara Karsavina in the original Ballet Russe production of "The Firebird."

degree *Oedipus Rex* and *Symphony of Psalms,* it is somewhat rare to hear his music performed in live concerts.

One reason may be that as a composer he was very different from others such as Tchaikovsky, his boyhood idol. Tchaikovsky poured out his feelings into his music. It is filled with memorable melodies that audiences enjoy hearing. But Stravinsky "never was a heart-on-sleeve composer, and often he cold-bloodedly discarded an obvious type of melody in favor of other elements of music," says Schonberg. "It may be that Stravinsky, 'the world's greatest living composer,' will end up living more for what he did to music rather than for what his music did to the majority of his listeners."[5]

That may be true. But no one will ever forget what his music did to his listeners on the night of May 29, 1913.

Born in Russia in 1884, Adolph Bolm (here shown as the Tsarevich in Stravinsky's Firebird *ballet), settled in the United States in 1916. He became a noted choreographer, spending many years with the American Ballet Theatre.*

GEORGE BALANCHINE

FYInfo

George Balanchine is considered one of the greatest ballet choreographers of the 20th century. A choreographer is the person who works out the steps of a dance. Balanchine was born in St. Petersburg, Russia, in 1904 and began playing the piano when he was five. Four years later he started taking ballet lessons. After graduating from the Imperial Ballet School in 1921, he joined the State Theater of Opera and Ballet. He also studied piano and music theory at the Petrograd Conservatory of Music. Meanwhile he began choreographing, first for himself and later for others.

Ballets Russes stages *Pulcinella*

Three years later, he moved to Paris and joined Serge Diaghilev in the Ballets Russes. A knee injury soon ended his career as a dancer, but by then he was well established as a choreographer. When Diaghilev died in 1929, the Ballets Russes disbanded. Balanchine spent five years working on a variety of projects in Europe. Lincoln Kirstein, a wealthy American, wanted to form an American ballet company that would be as good as the ones in Europe. In 1933, he met Balanchine and invited him to come the United States to form a ballet company. At first Balanchine was associated with the Metropolitan Opera, but in 1946 he founded what would become the New York City Ballet. It was where he would spend the rest of his life.

In 1954, Balanchine choreographed Peter Tchaikovsky's *Nutcracker.* That is generally regarded as starting the tradition of staging the *Nutcracker* during the holiday season. Since then, companies large and small all over the country have produced *Nutcracker*s at that time, earning a large portion of their annual operating expenses.

Balanchine also worked closely for many years with Stravinsky, choreographing such works as *Firebird, Renard, Orpheus, Agon, Variations for Orchestra,* and *Violin Concerto.*

By the time of his death in 1983, George Balanchine had choreographed nearly 500 ballets. During his lifetime, he received many honors. Perhaps the highest was the Presidential Medal of Freedom. It is the highest government honor that can be given to an American civilian.

Selected Works

Ballets
Firebird
Petrushka
The Rite of Spring
Pulcinella
The Fairy's Kiss
Apollon Musagète
Orpheus
Agon
Symphonies
Symphony in C
Symphony in Three Movements
Symphony of Psalms
Operas
The Nightingale
The Rake's Progress
Vocal Music
Oedipus Rex
Requiem Canticles
Orchestral Music
L'histoire du soldat (*A Soldier's Tale*)
Les Noces (The Wedding)
Ebony Concerto
Circus Polka

Chronology

1882 Born on June 17 in Oranienbaum (Lomonosov), Russia
1889 Attends first ballet
1893 Sees Peter Tchaikovsky at a concert
1901 Enters University of St. Petersburg as a law student
1902 Meets composer Nikolai Rimsky-Korsakov; father dies
1905 Finishes studies at University of St. Petersburg
1906 Marries cousin Catherine Nossenko
1907 Son Theodore born
1908 Daughter Lyudmila born
1909 Meets Sergei Diaghilev
1910 *Firebird* premieres; son Sviatoslav Soulima born
1911 *Petrushka* premieres
1913 *The Rite of Spring* premieres
1914 Moves to Switzerland; daughter Maria Milena born
1920 Moves to Paris
1934 Becomes French citizen
1938 Daughter Lyudmila dies
1939 Wife Catherine dies; mother dies; leaves France and comes to the United States
1940 Marries Vera de Bosset
1945 Becomes U.S. citizen
1962 Returns to Russia for first time in 48 years
1971 Dies on April 6 in New York City; his body is taken to Venice, Italy, for burial

Timeline in History

1804	Russian composer Mikhail Glinka is born.
1840	Russian composer Peter Tchaikovsky is born.
1857	Glinka dies.
1872	Russian ballet impresario Sergei Diaghilev is born.
1882	Future U.S. president Franklin Delano Roosevelt is born.
1883	New York City's Metropolitan Opera House opens.
1888	Composer Irving Berlin is born.
1892	Composer Peter Tchaikovsky's ballet *The Nutcracker* premieres.
1896	The first modern Olympic Games are held in Athens, Greece.
1901	Queen Victoria's death ends her 63-year reign, the longest in English history.
1905	Russian police brutally crush a street demonstration in what becomes known as Bloody Sunday.
1909	U.S. explorers Robert Peary and Matthew Henson become the first men to reach the North Pole.
1914	World War I begins; expected to be over within a few months, it lasts for more than four years.
1917	Czar Nicholas II of Russia gives up his throne; he and his family are murdered the following year.
1922	The Union of Soviet Socialist Republics (USSR), consisting of Russia and 14 other countries, is established under communist control.
1926	A. A. Milne publishes *Winnie the Pooh.*
1929	Sergei Diaghilev dies; stock market crash sends U.S. into Great Depression.
1933	Adolf Hitler becomes German chancellor; later that year the Enabling Law gives him dictatorial powers.
1935	The Baseball Hall of Fame is founded in Cooperstown, New York.
1938	German scientists Otto Hahn and Fritz Strassman split the atom, which leads to the development of the atomic bomb seven years later.
1945	World War II ends, and the United Nations is founded.
1951	Richard Rodgers and Oscar Hammerstein II premiere their musical *The King and I* on Broadway.
1957	USSR launches *Sputnik I* and *Sputnik II,* the first two artificial Earth satellites.
1963	U.S. President John F. Kennedy is assassinated.
1964	The Beatles appear on live U.S. television for the first time.
1969	American astronaut Neil Armstrong becomes the first person to set foot on the moon.
1971	U.S. jazz trumpeter Louis Armstrong dies.
1989	Composer Irving Berlin dies.
2002	The "Rolling Requiem" honors the victims of September 11, 2001: Choirs all around the world begin performing Mozart's *Requiem* at precisely 8:11 A.M. local time, the moment when one year before the first airliner hijacked by terrorists slammed into the World Trade Center in New York City.
2004	Ballet companies and other organizations across the United States celebrate the George Balanchine Centennial, the 100th anniversary of the great choreographer's birth.

Chapter Notes

Chapter 1 A Night to Remember

1. Stephen Walsh, *Stravinsky: A Creative Spring, Russia and France 1882–1934* (New York: Alfred A. Knopf, 1999), p. 203.
2. Igor Stravinsky, *An Autobiography* (New York: M. & J. Steuer, 1958), p. 47.
3. Phil G. Goulding, *Classical Music: The 50 Greatest Composers and Their 1,000 Greatest Works* (New York: Ballantine Books, 1992), p. 261.
4. Harold Schonberg, *The Lives of the Great Composers* (New York: W.W. Norton, 1981), p. 495.
5. Walsh, *Stravinsky*, p. 204.
6. Ibid.
7. Ibid.
8. Ibid., p. 206.
9. Ibid.
10. Ibid., p. 203.
11. Ibid., p. 206.

Chapter 2 The Budding Musician

1. Igor Stravinsky, *An Autobiography* (New York: M. & J. Steuer, 1958), p. 6.
2. Eric Walter White, *Stravinsky: The Composer and His Works* (Berkeley, Calif.: University of California Press, 1979), p. 23.
3. Stravinsky, *An Autobiography*, p. 7.

Chapter 3 Laying Down the Law

1. Igor Stravinsky, *An Autobiography* (New York: M. & J. Steuer, 1958), p. 8.
2. Ibid., p. 13.
3. Eric Walter White, *Stravinsky: The Composer and His Works* (Berkeley, Calif.: University of California Press, 1979), p. 25.
4. Stravinsky, *An Autobiography*, p. 15.

Chapter 4 Three Great Ballets

1. Harold Schonberg, *The Lives of the Great Composers* (New York: W.W. Norton, 1981), p. 495.
2. Roman Vlad, *Stravinsky,* translated by Frederick and Ann Fuller (London: Oxford University Press, 1960), p. 29.
3. Schonberg, *The Lives of the Great Composers*, p. 496.
4. Eric Walter White, *Stravinsky: The Composer and His Works* (Berkeley, Calif.: University of California Press, 1979), p. 48.
5. Stephen Walsh, *Stravinsky: A Creative Spring, Russia and France 1882–1934* (New York: Alfred A. Knopf, 1999), p. 232.

Chapter 5 Leaving His Homeland Behind

1. Eric Walter White, *Stravinsky: The Composer and His Works* (Berkeley, Calif.: University of California Press, 1979), p. 87.
2. Ibid., pp. 92–93.
3. Danceworks, "Le sacre du printemps" *(The Rite of Spring),* (http://www.danceworksonline.co.uk/sidesteps/people/stravinsky.htm, n.d.).
4. Harold Schonberg, *The Lives of the Great Composers* (New York: W.W. Norton, 1981), p. 505.
5. Ibid., pp. 505–506.

For Further Reading

For Young Adults

Cleaver, Elizabeth. *Petrouchka: Adapted from Igor Stravinsky and Alexandre Benois.* New York: Atheneum, 1980.

Ganeri, Anita. *The Young Person's Guide to the Ballet.* New York: Harcourt, 1998.

Vernon, Roland. *Introducing Stravinsky.* Broomall, Pa.: Chelsea House Publishers, 2001.

Yolen, Jane. *The Firebird.* New York: Harper Collins Children's Books, 2000.

Works Consulted

Goulding, Phil G. *Classical Music: The 50 Greatest Composers and Their 1,000 Greatest Works.* New York: Ballantine Books, 1992.

Griffiths, Paul. *The Master Musicians: Stravinsky.* New York: Schirmer Books, 1992.

Schonberg, Harold C. *The Lives of the Great Composers.* New York: W.W. Norton & Company, 1981.

Stravinsky, Igor. *An Autobiography.* New York: M. & J. Steuer, 1958.

Vlad, Roman. *Stravinsky.* Translated by Frederick and Ann Fuller. London: Oxford University Press, 1960.

Walsh, Stephen. *The New Grove Stravinsky.* New York: Palgrave, 2002.

———. *Stravinsky: A Creative Spring, Russia and France 1882–1934*. New York: Alfred A. Knopf, 1999.

White, Eric Walter. *Stravinsky: The Composer and His Works.* Berkeley, Calif.: University of California Press, 1979.

Young, Percy M. *Masters of Music: Stravinsky.* New York: Cornerstone Library, 1969.

On the Internet

Classical Music Pages, "Igor Stravinsky"
http://w3.rz-berlin.mpg.de/cmp/stravinsky.html

Danceworks, "Le sacre du printemps" *(The Rite of Spring)*
http://www.danceworksonline.co.uk/sidesteps/roots/riteofspring2.htm

Danceworks, Igor Fyodorovich Stravinsky
http://www.danceworksonline.co.uk/sidesteps/people/stravinsky.htm

Tim Dirks, "Fantasia (1940)"
http://www.filmsite.org/fant.html

Ziggy's Video Realm, "Fantasia"
http://www.reelcriticism.com/ziggyrealm/reviews/fantasia.html

Andreas Teuber, "Robert Louis Stevenson"
http://people.brandeis.edu/-teuber/stevensonbio.html#MainEssaySection

"Robert Louis Stevenson, Life and Works Outline"
http://wwwesterni.unibg.it/rls/bio.htm

Albert Schweitzer: Doctor, Musician, Theologian
http://home.pcisys.net/-jnf/sidebar.html

Nobel e-Museum, "Albert Schweitzer—Biography"
http://www.nobel.se/peace/laureates/1952/schweitzer-bio.html

Michael Morrison, "Fall of the Hindenburg"
http://www.infoplease.com/spot/hindenburg1.html

U.S. Centennial of Flight Commission, "The Zeppelin"
http://www.centennialofflight.gov/essay/Lighter_than_air/zeppelin/LTA8.htm

"George Balanchine"
http://en2.wikipedia.org/wiki/George_Balanchine

New York City Ballet, About NYCB, "George Balanchine 1904–1983"
http://www.nycballet.com/about/nycbgbbio.html

Index